WORDS YOU DON'T WANT TO HEAR DURING YOUR ANNUAL PERFORMANCE REVIEW

Other DILBERT books from Andrews McMeel Publishing

When Body Language Goes Bad
ISBN: 0-7407-3298-6

What Do You Call a Sociopath in a Cubicle?
Answer: A Coworker
ISBN: 0-7407-2663-3

Another Day in Cubicle Paradise
ISBN: 0-7407-2194-1

When Did Ignorance Become a Point of View?
ISBN: 0-7407-1839-8

Excuse Me While I Wag
ISBN: 0-7407-1390-6

Dilbert—A Treasury of Sunday Strips: Version 00
ISBN: 0-7407-0531-8

Random Acts of Management
ISBN: 0-7407-0453-2

Dilbert Gives You the Business
ISBN: 0-7407-0338-2 hardcover
ISBN: 0-7407-0003-0 paperback

Don't Step in the Leadership
ISBN: 0-8362-7844-5

Journey to Cubeville
ISBN: 0-8362-7175-0 hardcover
ISBN: 0-8362-6745-1 paperback

I'm Not Anti-Business, I'm Anti-Idiot
ISBN: 0-8362-5182-2

Seven Years of Highly Defective People
ISBN: 0-8362-5129-6 hardcover
ISBN: 0-8362-3668-8 paperback

Casual Day Has Gone Too Far
ISBN: 0-8362-2899-5

Fugitive from the Cubicle Police
ISBN: 0-8362-2119-2

Still Pumped from Using the Mouse
ISBN: 0-8362-1026-3

It's Obvious You Won't Survive by Your Wits Alone
ISBN: 0-8362-0415-8

Bring Me the Head of Willy the Mailboy!
ISBN: 0-8362-1779-9

Shave the Whales
ISBN: 0-8362-1740-3

Dogbert's Clues for the Clueless
ISBN: 0-8362-1737-3

Build a Better Life by Stealing Office Supplies
ISBN: 0-8362-1757-8

Always Postpone Meetings with Time-Wasting Morons
ISBN: 0-8362-1758-6

For ordering information, call 1-800-223-2336.

WORDS YOU DON'T WANT TO HEAR DURING YOUR ANNUAL PERFORMANCE REVIEW

A DILBERT™ BOOK
BY SCOTT ADAMS

**Andrews McMeel
Publishing**

Kansas City

03 04 05 06 07 BBG 10 9 8 7 6 5 4 3 2 1

ISBN: 0-7407-3805-4

Library of Congress Control Number: 2003106552

www.dilbert.com

For the Queen of Imaginary Quilts

Introduction

If you are an "employee," sooner or later you will be subjected to a horrible humiliation that forensic scientists refer to as your "performance review." You will need a strategy for coping, and I can help.

I recommend working for a timid boss who likes to avoid confrontation. You can test whether your boss fits that description by bringing a huge bag of fertilizer to work and shoving his head into it, then sewing it to his shirt collar and laughing as he goes running around like a man with a bag-o-fertilizer head.

After that, if he says something about how humor helps morale and how you're like a member of the family, then you have a timid boss, and your performance review will be just fine. He'll give you "exceptional" ratings on every category just to lessen the chance you will cry, complain, glare, or sew his head into another bag.

The next best kind of boss is a lazy boss. If he asks you to write your own performance review, you're home free. Try to weave into your evaluation words like *Einsteinian, overlord, magnificent,* and *deeeee-licious.* Even if he crosses out a few of your descriptors, whatever slips through the cracks will still serve you well.

If your boss is neither timid nor lazy, you'll have to do things the hard way. Sacrifice your health and your personal life by working extra hard to earn that highest performance review rating. Bankers will tell you that the 1 percent higher raise you earn for being a star performer will add up over time, thanks to the miracle of compounding. But later, when they're alone, the bankers will laugh heartily at your working 50 percent harder for a 1 percent higher raise. And they'll mock you for not understanding that compounding doesn't apply to people who spend all their extra money on beer to forget their jobs. Bankers are funny.

Or you could ignore your performance review altogether, and wait until Dogbert conquers the planet and makes all non-*Dilbert*-readers our personal domestic servants. To become a member of Dogbert's New Ruling Class (DNRC), and get the free *Dilbert Newsletter* that is published approximately whenever I feel like it, go to www.dilbert.com and follow the subscription instructions. If that doesn't work for some reason, send an e-mail to newsletter@unitedmedia.com.

S.Adams

SWEET MOTHER OF POTATOES! I JUST THOUGHT OF A BILLION-DOLLAR IDEA!!

THE COMPANY OWNS ALL OF YOUR IDEAS. COUGH IT UP OR I'LL FIRE YOU AND THEN SUE YOU.

YOUR FIRST BILLION-DOLLAR IDEA IS ALWAYS THE HARDEST.

WAAA!

CAROL, I'M SENDING YOU TO AN EXECUTIVE BODYGUARD CLASS.

YOU'LL LEARN HOW TO POUNCE ON A KIDNAPPER AND SACRIFICE YOURSELF TO KEEP ME SAFE.

I'M TAKING A CLASS CALLED "INSIDE HELP."

I CAN'T REIMBURSE FOR THAT.

I HAVE MAIL! I'VE NEVER HAD MAIL IN TWELVE YEARS HERE.

IT'S NOT ADDRESSED TO ME BUT IT WAS IN MY BOX SO I'M KEEPING IT.

NO MAIL FOR TWELVE YEARS?

IF I HOLD IT JUST RIGHT IT GLISTENS.

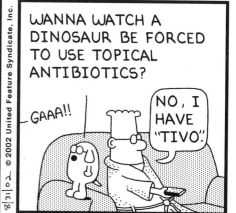

13

THIS IS OUR NEW CEO, RUFUS T. SKWERREL. HIS FIRST JOB WAS TRAILER PARK BURGLAR.

BUT THANKS TO A SERIES OF MERGERS AND ACQUISITIONS, NOT TO MENTION SUSPICIOUS ACCOUNTING, HERE WE ARE.

WOULD YOU LIKE TO SAY A FEW WORDS?

WALLET AND WATCH.

I LIKE OUR NEW CEO. HE HAS CHARISMA.

THE MAN SURE KNOWS HOW TO ROB. HE'S A MIRACLE WORKER WITH DUCT TAPE.

HE EVEN GAVE ME BACK MY EMPTIED WALLET.

CLASSY MOVE.

THEN OUR NEW CEO BACKED UP A MOVING VAN TO THE BUILDING AND ROBBED US.

AT FIRST WE THOUGHT HE WAS BREAKING THE LAW, BUT HE HAD A WRITTEN OPINION FROM HIS TAX LAWYER SAYING IT WAS PROBABLY OKAY.

WHAT DID THE BOARD OF DIRECTORS DO?

AFTER LOADING THE VAN?

OUR DRESS CODE POLICY WILL GO BACK TO BUSINESS ATTIRE.

AND I WILL KEEP CHANGING THE DRESS CODE UNTIL I FIND THE CLOTHING STYLE THAT MAKES OUR PROFITS GO UP!

LATER, AT THE SARTORIAL ALCHEMY LAB

WATCH OUT. THIS MIGHT SPARK.

DILBERT, MEET A WOMAN WHO ACTS PEEVED AT ANY SORT OF QUESTION.

HOW ARE YOU?

POINK

HOW AM I ???

WOW. I GOTTA SHOW THIS TO WALLY.

GRAB YOUR DENTAL FLOSS AND FOLLOW ME. I'LL EXPLAIN ON THE WAY.

OKAY.

THE NEWLY HIRED MUTANT IS NAMED "PEEVED EVE." WAIT UNTIL YOU SEE HER PEEVED EXPRESSION.

HEE HEE!

GAAA! PUBLIC FLOSSING!

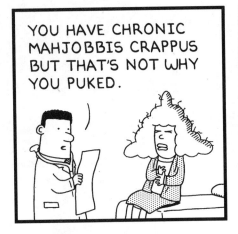

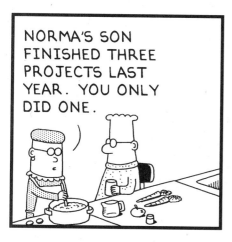

NORMA'S SON FINISHED THREE PROJECTS LAST YEAR. YOU ONLY DID ONE.

HIS CUBICLE IS A DOUBLE-WIDE. AND HIS CEO ONCE SAID HI TO HIM IN THE ELEVATOR.

THANKS TO YOU, MY "SCRABBLE" NIGHT IS A LIVING HELL.

DO YOU STILL USE COUNTERFEIT VOWELS?

WHY HAVE YOU ONLY FINISHED ONE PROJECT AT WORK THIS YEAR? NORMA'S SON DID THREE.

YOU CAN'T MEASURE SOMEONE'S WORTH BY COUNTING THE NUMBER OF PROJECTS HE DOES.

MAYBE WE SHOULD TRACK ROI INSTEAD.

WHY, BECAUSE YOU'RE LOSING?

IN SCHOOL, I WAS ALWAYS THE LAST KID PICKED TO BE ON A TEAM.

I NEED TWO PEOPLE RIGHT NOW. I'LL TAKE ASOK AND... I'LL KEEP LOOKING.

SO IT'S LIKE A SUPER POWER?

PRETTY MUCH.

26

DILBERT, I WANT YOU TO INTEGRATE OUR SALES DATABASE WITH OUR INVENTORY AND FINANCE SYSTEMS.

THE MANAGERS OF THOSE SYSTEMS ARE A NITWIT, AN OGRE, AND A $#!$%, RESPECTIVELY.

AND THEY KNOW THAT TWO OF THEM WILL BE FIRED WHEN IT'S COMPLETE.

I CAN GET THAT DONE IN THIRTY YEARS.

OUR PROJECT TEAM IS COMPOSED OF A NITWIT, AN OGRE, AND A #$$%!

WHICH ONE OF THEM IS THE NITWIT?

YOU DIDN'T BRING DONUTS. MAY I EAT THE NITWIT?

YES.

POOR GUY.

MY PROJECT IS STALLED BECAUSE MY NITWIT HATES MY OGRE, AND MY #$$%! WON'T DO ANY WORK.

MY OGRE ATE MY NITWIT AND MY #$$%! IS TRYING TO BLAME ME FOR IT.

DO YOU WANT TO BORROW MY NITWIT?

NO, I HAVE A REQUISITION IN.

29

A SURVEY OF YOUR TV AD EFFECTIVENESS SHOWS THAT NO ONE HAS HEARD OF YOUR COMPANY.

YOUR AD ONLY SAYS YOUR NAME ONCE, AT THE END OF A BORING COMMERCIAL WHEN VIEWERS HAVE DRIFTED OFF.

I RECOMMEND THROWING YOUR AD MONEY INTO A SPECIAL KIND OF HOLE.

WHEN CAN WE START?

RATBERT, I NEED YOU TO DIG A HUGE RAT HOLE, SO COMPANIES CAN THROW MONEY IN IT.

YES!!!

I MIGHT SHARE SOME OF THE MONEY WITH YOU.

YOU HAD ME AT "HOLE."

WHEN SHOULD I STOP DIGGING?

WHEN YOU SMELL FEET.

MAY I THROW MONEY DOWN THE RAT HOLE?

SHOW ME YOUR BUSINESS PLAN.

RAT HOLE →

$

YOU PLAN TO PAY HUGE INVESTMENT BANKING FEES TO BUY A LOW-MARGIN, MONEY-LOSING BUSINESS...

FOR AN EXTRA FEE, I'LL PUSH YOU IN THE HOLE AND TAKE YOUR MONEY.

OOOH, SOUNDS GOOD.

$

35

36

38

MOM, I'LL GET FIRED UNLESS YOU DROP YOUR LAWSUIT AGAINST MY COMPANY.

WHY DO YOU WORK FOR A COMPANY THAT'S MANAGED BY DESPICABLE WEASELS?

THEY TELL ME IT'S BECAUSE I ENJOY THE CHALLENGE.

I DEMAND A DNA TEST.

DOGBERT THE ATTORNEY

YOUR BEST DEFENSE IS TO SAY YOU WERE IGNORANT OF YOUR COMPANY'S STOCK MANIPULATION.

WE NEED TO CONVINCE A JUDGE THAT YOU'RE DUMBER THAN CHOCOLATE PANTS AT AN OUTDOOR LAS VEGAS PHOTOGRAPHY CONVENTION.

I DON'T GET THAT.

E-E-EXCELLENT.

I WILL PROVE THAT MY CLIENT IS TOO DUMB TO EMBEZZLE.

OR, FAILING IN THAT, I'LL PROVE THAT YOU'RE TOO DUMB TO KNOW HE DID IT.

MISTER DOGBERT...

DON'T GET ME STARTED ABOUT YOU.

WE FIND THE DEFENDANT GUILTY AND WE SENTENCE HIM TO DEATH.

UMM...WE HAVEN'T DELIBERATED. WE HAVEN'T EVEN HEARD ANY EVIDENCE YET.

OKAY, SO, WHAT I'M HEARING IS THAT LENO'S MONOLOGUE IS NOT EVIDENCE?

DOGBERT THE ATTORNEY

YOUR HONOR, IS IT TOO LATE TO CHANGE SIDES?

AFTER HEARING THE EVIDENCE, I WANT TO PUNISH MY CLIENT.

NO?

I EXPECT SOME AWKWARD SILENCES DURING THE NEXT BREAK.

THE COURT FINDS YOU GUILTY OF DEFRAUDING STOCKHOLDERS.

YOU WILL SERVE YOUR TIME IN A PLACE SO HORRIBLE THAT IT HAS NO NAME.

HERE'S YOUR ROOMIE.

BURP

I'M A TEMP WITH A FEAR OF COMMITMENT. I KEEP ONE FOOT OUT THE DOOR.

WHATEVER. JUST TAKE CARE OF THIS FOR ME. IT'LL TAKE TEN MINUTES.

ZIP

I'VE DEVELOPED A NEW THEORY OF INTELLIGENCE THAT I CALL "DROP-BY I.Q."

IT'S A MEASURE OF HOW LONG A DROP-BY VISITOR WILL STAY IN YOUR CUBICLE WHEN YOU'RE TRYING TO WORK

ONE HOUR AND COUNTING.

...AND THAT'S WHY I'M AFRAID OF BANANAS.

DON'T GIVE PERFORMANCE REVIEWS ON TIME.

WAIT UNTIL AN EMPLOYEE SCREWS UP SOMETHING BIG, THEN POUNCE!

...I FORGOT TO UNPLUG THE DEMO UNIT AND IT BURNED DOWN OUR CUSTOMER'S HEADQUARTERS.

DO YOU HAVE A MINUTE?

44

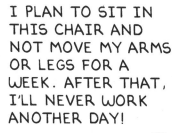

THE SHORT-TIMER

HOW WILL YOU LEAVE IF YOU REFUSE TO USE ANY MAJOR MUSCLE GROUPS UNTIL RETIREMENT?

I'M HOPING SOMEONE WILL BUY ME A MOTORIZED WHEELCHAIR AND LIFT ME INTO IT.

I WOULD BE WILLING TO DRAG YOU TO THE CURB.

FACE UP?

THERE'S AN EMERGENCY STRATEGY MEETING IN FIVE MINUTES.

I WAS ALL WARM AND COZY IN MY CUBICLE PARADISE. WHY MUST YOU RUIN IT?

CAN YOU HEAR THE SOUND OF ME NOT CARING?

WE NEED A CLEAR STRATEGY. DOES ANYONE HAVE A SUGGESTION?

LET'S FIGURE OUT WHAT MAKES US THE MOST PROFIT, AND THEN DO MORE OF IT.

IT NEEDS TO BE LESS CLEAR THAN THAT.

CAN IT BE ILLEGAL?

THE MARKETING DEPARTMENT WANTS YOU TO BUILD A DEVICE THAT TURNS CUSTOMERS INTO SHEEP.

WHY? SO THEY'LL BUY WHATEVER WE TELL THEM TO BUY?

TO BE HONEST, WE HAVEN'T GIVEN IT MUCH THOUGHT BEYOND FREE WOOL.

MY INVENTION WILL TURN PEOPLE INTO MINDLESS SHEEP.

I'M CURIOUS HOW YOU'LL KNOW IT WORKS. I ASSUME IT'S MOSTLY A COSMETIC CHANGE.

DOGBERT, DID YOU UNPLUG IT AS I ASKED YOU?

COULDN'T BE BOTHERED.

A LAB ACCIDENT TURNED ME INTO A SHEEP.

IT'S NOT ALL BAD. IN ADDITION TO BEING SOFT AND WARM, I NEVER NEED TO FORM OPINIONS.

IF YOU WANT SOME WOOL, JUST GRAB ME AND START SHAVING. I'LL BARELY STRUGGLE.

COOL!

MY MAGNETIC-CANCEL-LATION WHEEL WILL CREATE UNLIMITED FREE ENERGY.

BUWAHAHA!!!

I WILL USE THIS TECHNOLOGY TO RULE THE WORLD!!!

UM... IT'S NOT YOURS.

WHAT TIME ARE YOU GOING TO BED?

MY DREAM WAS TO SOMEDAY DECOMPOSE AND BECOME FOSSIL FUEL.

BUT DILBERT'S CRUEL INVENTION WILL MAKE FUEL UNNECESSARY. NOW MY LIFE HAS NO PURPOSE!

YOU CAN BE MY DISPOSABLE EVIL LACKEY.

I-I-I CAN?

WE'LL ARTIFICIALLY BOOST REVENUES BY SELLING TO OUR OWN OFFSHORE SUBSIDIARY.

THEN WE'LL BOOK OUR EXPENSES AS CAPITAL, LIE TO THE MEDIA ABOUT OUR PROSPECTS, BRIBE AN INDUSTRY ANALYST, AND CASH OUT!

I KNOW I'M DOING SOMETHING RIGHT WHEN MY BUSINESS PRACTICES GAG A RAT.

AAK AAK AAK

THE REPORTER FROM MONEYBAGS MAGAZINE IS HERE.

SEND HIM IN.

ARE YOU PLANNING TO ASK MY EMPLOYEES IF MY CLAIMS ARE TRUE?

NAH, TOO LAZY.

I CREDIT MY SUCCESS TO THE FOOT MASSAGES I PERSONALLY GIVE TO EACH EMPLOYEE.

COVER STORY!

I SOLD MY STOCK AND MADE BILLIONS BEFORE DRIVING MY COMPANY INTO BANKRUPTCY.

NOW I DO THE WEASEL DANCE. HOO-AH! YEE-HA! WOO-WOO-WOO!

WOULD IT KILL YOU TO CLAP AND SING ALONG?

THEN THEY RIP OUT YOUR EGO AND THEY PUT YOU IN A BOX UNTIL YOU ROT!!

GAAA!!

YOU'LL NEVER KNOW IF YOU'RE DEAD OR IF YOU'RE SIMPLY ENVYING THE DEAD!!

HOW WAS "CAREER DAY"?

KIDS THESE DAYS ARE AFRAID OF WORK.

I CALCULATED THE IMPACT OF WORK ON MY HEALTH AND LIFE EXPECTANCY.

AT MY CURRENT WORKLOAD, DOING TWO PEOPLE'S JOBS, I HAVE...SIX MONTHS TO LIVE.

REMIND ME IN FIVE AND A HALF MONTHS SO I CAN SHOP FOR A CARD.

ESTATE PLANNING

I EXPECT TO WORK MYSELF TO DEATH IN SIX MONTHS, SO I NEED A WILL.

ARE YOU MENTALLY INCOMPETENT?

I DON'T THINK SO.

OKAY THEN, I'LL REMOVE MY NAME FROM THE LIST OF BENEFICIARIES.

ESTATE PLANNING

YOU CAN AVOID PROBATE COSTS BY CREATING A LIVING TRUST.

SO...I CAN USE AN INCONVENIENT SYSTEM CREATED BY LAWYERS TO AVOID A WORSE SYSTEM CREATED BY LAWYERS?

ACCORDING TO MY WATCH, THAT WITTY OBSERVATION COST YOU FOUR DOLLARS.

QUIT STARING. I OVERSLEPT AND NOW I HAVE A BAD CASE OF BED HAIR.

I'M CONFUSED. SURELY IT WOULD HAVE GONE BACK TO NORMAL AFTER YOUR SHOWER.

PLEASE DO NOT UNLEASH THE UNHYGIENIC FIST OF DEATH!

PERFORMANCE REVIEW

YOU DID TWO JOBS FOR A YEAR AND DID THEM WELL.

I HAVE NO BUDGET FOR RAISES, SO ALL I CAN OFFER IS AN ATTABOY.

THE PROBLEM IS: I DON'T WANT TO CHEAPEN THE WHOLE ATTABOY SYSTEM.

I CAN MONITOR ALL EMPLOYEE E-MAIL FROM HERE.

I'M LOOKING FOR RECENTLY ESTRANGED LOVERS SO I CAN PROMOTE ONE OF THEM OVER THE OTHER.

WHY IS MY NEW JOB TITLE A LONG STRING OF CURSE WORDS?

I WIN.

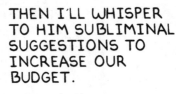

MAKE YOUR "POWER-POINT" PRESENTATION SO BORING THAT OUR CEO WILL SLIP INTO A TRANCE.

THEN I'LL WHISPER TO HIM SUBLIMINAL SUGGESTIONS TO INCREASE OUR BUDGET.

MORE BUDGET.

KILL THE POINTY-HAIRED MONSTER

BOB WILL DEMON-STRATE OUR NEW BIOMETRIC SECU-RITY SYSTEM.

THE SYSTEM CHECKS FOR PULSE, HEAT AND FINGERPRINTS TO IDENTIFY EACH EMPLOYEE.

IT SAYS I DON'T HAVE ANY OF THOSE THINGS.

ARE YOU THE ONE THEY CALL WALLY?

FOR THOUSANDS OF GENERATIONS THE MALES IN MY FAMILY PRACTICED SELECTIVE BREEDING.

THE GOAL WAS TO PRODUCE OFFSPRING THAT LEAVE NO BIO-METRIC IMPRESSION: NO PULSE, NO FINGER-PRINTS, NO DNA.

WHY?

WE LIKE TO ASK "WHY NOT?"

MY PLAN IS TO SELL LOW-COST VIDEO-PHONES TO DIM-WITTED IDENTICAL TWINS.

I'LL EVEN THROW IN FREE LONG-DISTANCE CALLING BECAUSE THAT'S THE KIND OF GUY I AM.

GAAA!!! WHAT ARE YOU DOING AT MY GIRLFRIEND'S HOUSE???

1/2/03 © 2002 United Feature Syndicate, Inc.

A REPORTER WANTS TO SEE YOU.

HE CLAIMS WE'VE BEEN DELIVERING ALL OF OUR GARBAGE TO THE LOCAL PARK FOR TWENTY YEARS.

HOW IS THAT EVEN POSSIBLE?

THE SECRET IS IN THE SPREADING.

1/3/03 © 2002 United Feature Syndicate, Inc.

INVESTIGATIVE REPORTER

EXPLAIN WHY YOUR COMPANY DUMPS GARBAGE IN THE PARK.

AND WHY DO YOU DRIVE SUCH A HUGE, WASTEFUL VEHICLE?

I NEED YOU TO SCRAPE SOMETHING OFF MY TIRES AND TAKE IT TO THE PARK.

1/4/03 © 2002 United Feature Syndicate, Inc.

I NEED YOUR SELF-EVALUATION SO I CAN WRITE YOUR PERFORMANCE REVIEW.

REMEMBER TO RATE YOURSELF ON OUR CORE VALUES OF HONESTY AND INTEGRITY.

WALLY CLAIMS HE DID NO WORK THIS YEAR. BUT HE'S DISHONEST, SO YOU CAN'T BE SURE.

ALL SHREDDERS ARE BEING CENTRALIZED AT OUR CORPORATE HEADQUARTERS.

IF YOU NEED SOMETHING SHREDDED, GIVE IT TO ASOK.

DUDE, I THINK HE MEANT YOU WOULD TAKE IT TO THE SHREDDERS.

MOUTH... SO... DRY

HOW DO I MAKE THIS SOFTWARE SCHEDULE ONE PERSON TO TWO TASKS AT THE SAME TIME?

I CAN WRITE A PATCH THAT INSERTS NEW MONTHS IN THE TIMELINE.

AND THE SECOND TASK IS DUE ON THE FIFTEENTH OF FLOOPUARY.

WE'RE GOING TO TRY SOMETHING CALLED EXTREME PROGRAMMING.

FIRST, PICK A PARTNER. THE TWO OF YOU WILL WORK AT ONE COMPUTER FOR FORTY HOURS A WEEK.

THE NEW SYSTEM IS A MINUTE OLD AND I ALREADY HATE EVERYONE.

EXTREME PROGRAMMING

I CAN'T GIVE YOU ALL OF THESE FEATURES IN THE FIRST VERSION.

AND EACH FEATURE NEEDS TO HAVE WHAT WE CALL A "USER STORY."

OKAY, HERE'S A STORY: YOU GIVE ME ALL OF MY FEATURES OR I'LL RUIN YOUR LIFE.

EXTREME PROGRAMMING

THE TWO OF YOU WILL BE A CODE-WRITING TEAM.

STUDIES PROVE THAT TWO PROGRAMMERS ON ONE COMPUTER IS THE MOST PRODUCTIVE ARRANGEMENT.

SOMETIMES I CAN WHISTLE THROUGH BOTH NOSTRILS. I'VE SAVED A FORTUNE IN HARMONICAS.

HELLO, POTENTIAL CLIENT. I'M A CONSULTICK.

I'LL BURROW INTO YOUR CORPORATE SKIN, SUCK YOUR CASH AND NEVER LEAVE.

MY FIRM HAS A TRACK RECORD OF HUGE CONSULTING FAILURES AND CONFLICTS OF INTEREST!

NO RED FLAGS.

THE CONSULTICK

HE'LL DO MORE THAN GIVE US BAD ADVICE...

HE'LL ALSO MAKE SURE WE CAN'T IMPLEMENT IT WITHOUT HIM.

HA HA! NOW HE'S BURROWING INTO MY TORSO, AND I'VE CONVINCED MYSELF IT'S OKAY.

IT LOOKS LIKE YOU NEED "DOGBERT'S CONSULTANT REMOVAL SERVICE."

HE'S IN THERE GOOD. YOU MUST BE LOSING A LOT OF CASH.

IT ALREADY SPREAD TO YOUR WALLET. I'LL HAVE TO OPERATE IMMEDIATELY.

75

THE PROJECT IS BEHIND SCHEDULE BECAUSE OUR CONTRACTOR IS A LAZY BEAVER.

FOR A WHILE HE WAS MAKING UP EXCUSES. NOW, HE DOESN'T RETURN CALLS.

WHAT'S YOUR PLAN?

I HOPE TO GET HIM BACK TO MAKING UP EXCUSES BY PROMISING HIM MORE JOBS IN THE FUTURE.

WE NEED TO UPGRADE OUR PC OPERATING SYSTEMS, SO WE HAVE A STABLE ENVIRONMENT FOR APPLICATIONS.

THINK OF IT AS A FORM OF TAXATION BY AN EVIL SHADOW GOVERNMENT.

SHADOW GOVERNMENT? THAT'S RIDICULOUS.

SHUT UP AND PAY ME.

FOR ONLY A MILLION DOLLARS, YOU CAN UPGRADE TO OUR NEWEST SOFTWARE VERSION.

OR YOU CAN SLOWLY DECOMPOSE IN THE MIASMA OF OUR PLANNED OBSOLESCENCE.

WE CAN'T AFFORD TO UPGRADE NOW.

SAY GOODBYE TO THE DIGITS THREE AND NINE.

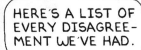

80

MY PROJECT IS IN A FLAMING DEATH SPIRAL, THANKS TO YOU LAZY, SELFISH WEASELS.

BUT I'M FEELING TERRIFIC BECAUSE I'M TAKING MOOD-ALTERING PRESCRIPTION DRUGS!

I CAN SEE BY YOUR EXPRESSIONS THAT MY DOCTOR IS MUCH BETTER THAN YOURS!

HOO-WAH!

THE PRESCRIPTION DRUGS MAKE ME HAPPY, BUT I WORRY THAT IT'S NOT GENUINE HAPPINESS.

ASK YOUR DOCTOR FOR A DRUG THAT CURES WORRYING. THEN YOU'LL HAVE IT ALL.

IT MIGHT MAKE YOU GROW AN EXOSKELETON, BUT YOU WON'T CARE.

COOL.

MY MEDICATION MAKES ME CAREFREE AND HAPPY, BUT THE SIDE EFFECT IS AN EXOSKELETON.

REMEMBER THE OLD SAYING — "BEAUTY IS ONLY BONE DEEP."

HEE HEE

BUT ENOUGH ABOUT ME. I DON'T WANT TO LOOK SHELLFISH.

YOU HAD A CHANCE UNTIL THE PUN.

83

MY MEDICATION MAKES ME HAPPY DESPITE MY EXOSKELETON, BAD JOB, AND SOCIAL LIFE.

IF CHEMICALS CAN CHANGE THE WAY I THINK AND WHAT I ENJOY, THEN FREE WILL MUST BE AN ILLUSION.

WHAT ABOUT YOUR SOUL?

I'M AN ENGINEER.

I HEARD YOU HAD A COLD.

IT WASN'T A COLD.

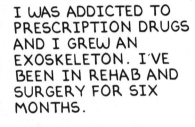

I WAS ADDICTED TO PRESCRIPTION DRUGS AND I GREW AN EXOSKELETON. I'VE BEEN IN REHAB AND SURGERY FOR SIX MONTHS.

JUST TO BE CLEAR: CAN I CATCH ANY OF THAT BY TOUCHING THE COFFEEMAKER AFTER YOU?

EVIL H.R. DIRECTOR

I NEED TO CHECK A FEW THINGS BEFORE WE HIRE YOU.

GIVE ME BLOOD, HAIR, AND URINE SAMPLES, FINGER-PRINTS, SOCIAL-SECURITY NUMBER, PAST EMPLOYERS, AND PAST LOVERS.

BEFORE WE STARTED DOING ALL OF THIS CHECKING, DID YOU KNOW THAT EVERYONE IN THE WORLD WAS DESPICABLE?

YES

86

I HAVE AN ASSIGNMENT FOR YOU THAT HAS NO VALUE WHATSOEVER TO THE COMPANY.

FOR REASONS OF COMPANY POLITICS, I NEED TO PRETEND I'M DOING SOMETHING IN THAT AREA.

SO, YOU'RE DOING ACTUAL WORK. WHAT'S THAT ALL ABOUT?

I HAVE AN APPOINTMENT TO SEE A DEMO OF YOUR NEW PRODUCT.

AND THE UNIT WILL BE IN A CASE LIKE THIS, BUT COMPLETELY DIFFERENT, AND IT WILL HAVE SOFTWARE, ONCE WE WRITE IT.

YOU LET ME TRAVEL FOUR HOURS TO SEE AN EMPTY CASE?

ARE YOU FORGETTING THE BLANK CD?

HOW OFTEN WOULD YOU CHARGE US THIS "ANNUAL FEE"?

IS THAT A JOKE?

SADLY, NO.

ONCE A MONTH.

SOUNDS FAIR.

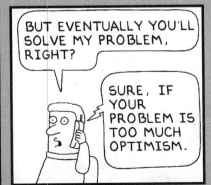

YOU DON'T RESPOND TO MY E-MAIL ANY-MORE.

WHEN I REPLY TO E-MAIL, IT ATTRACTS MORE E-MAIL. I'M TRYING TO BREAK THE VICIOUS CYCLE.

WELL...I'LL LEAVE YOU VOICE-MAILS.

LET ME KNOW HOW THAT WORKS OUT FOR YOU.

OUR FACILITIES MANAGEMENT SAYS THE NEW STATUE BY THE FRONT ENTRANCE ISN'T A STATUE.

IT'S AN UNLUCKY GUY NAMED KARL WHO HAD BEEN WARNED MANY TIMES NOT TO FEED THE BIRDS.

THEN IT TALKS ABOUT STATISTICAL CLUSTERING...BLAH, BLAH, BLAH...AND SERVING AS AN EXAMPLE.

I'VE DECIDED TO ADD CHRONIC LATENESS TO MY REPERTOIRE.

I'LL START WITH THE CLASSIC EXCUSES: CAR PROBLEMS, TRAFFIC, AND MISPLACED ITEMS. THEN I'LL BRANCH OUT.

YOU'RE THE MAYOR OF LOSERVILLE.

DON'T JINX IT.

WOULD YOU LIKE TO BUY SOME LIFE INSURANCE?

EXCLUSIONS: SELF-INFLICTED WOUNDS, PRE-EXISTING ILLNESS, CRIMINAL ACTS, WAR, DANGEROUS SPORTS, SMOKING...

MUCH LATER THAT DAY

...AND PISTOL DUELS RESULTING FROM QUILTING BEES.

NO ONE READS IT, FREAK!

CAROL, WHERE'S MY TEN O'CLOCK?

HE SAID HE'D BE LATE BECAUSE YOU'RE A MORON AND HE DOESN'T RESPECT YOU.

DID YOU TELL HIM I WAS STUCK IN TRAFFIC?

IT'S NOT ALWAYS ABOUT YOU.

WHY ISN'T MY CELL PHONE WORKING?

THAT'S A SHORT-RANGE CELL PHONE. YOU NEED TO BE IN THE SAME ROOM WITH THE PERSON YOU CALL.

ANSWER THE STINKIN' PHONE, ALICE.

WHY ARE YOU LISTENING TO A TV REMOTE CONTROL?

WALLY HAS BEEN RESEARCHING GREEK WORDS TO NAME OUR NEW PRODUCT.

ALL I HAVE IS ZEUS, AND PARTHENON, AND THE WORD "GREEK" ITSELF.

I UNDERSTAND THEY HAVE A WORD FOR A SPORTS EVENT, TOO. I'M TRYING TO TRACK THAT DOWN.

MY COMPANY IS MOVING TO A "JUST IN TIME" INVENTORY STRATEGY. YOU'LL DELIVER WHEN WE NEED IT.

SO...YOUR SUCCESS DEPENDS ON MY COMPANY DOING WHAT IT PROMISES? YOU HAVE MY DEEPEST SYMPATHY.

I FEEL A SHARP, STABBING PAIN IN MY CHEST.

AND SO IT BEGINS.

A CUSTOMER KEEPS ASKING WHEN WE'LL DELIVER THE STUFF THEY BOUGHT.

WHEN WILL WE?

NEVER. YOU LIED TO THEM TO GET THEIR BUSINESS.

YOU TOOK THEIR MONEY AND GAVE THEM NOTHING. DO YOU KNOW WHAT THAT MAKES YOU?

THE WINNER!

98

LET'S BRAINSTORM IDEAS FOR "EMPLOYEE MORALE-ENHANCEMENT DAY."

WE COULD PLAY "PIN THE TAIL ON THE POINTY-HAIRED WEASEL WHOSE BREATH SMELLS LIKE FEET."

WE MIGHT NEED MORE MORALE-ENHANCEMENT DAYS.

HOW ABOUT THIS WEEKEND WHEN I'M NOT HERE?

MARKETING GENIUS

WE DESIGNED A REBATE PROGRAM THAT WON'T COST A PENNY.

THE REBATE PROCESS IS AN IMPENETRABLE FORTRESS OF UNCLEAR INSTRUCTIONS AND PHYSICAL IMPOSSI-BILITIES.

NEXT WE HAVE TO FIND THE HIDDEN 300-DIGIT SERIAL NUMBER AND WRITE IT IN A BOX THAT'S HALF AN INCH LONG.

STINKIN' WEASELS.

THE DEPARTMENT THAT CUTS COSTS THE MOST WILL GET OUR CEO AS ITS SECRETARY FOR A DAY.

I'M DEEPLY OFFENDED BY THE IMPLICATION THAT MY JOB IS SO TRIVIAL THAT IT CAN BE USED AS A PRIZE.

MAYBE YOU CAN TRAIN HIM TO PHONE YOUR KIDS AND YELL AT THEM.

NOT FUNNY!!

OUR DEPARTMENT WON THE COST-CUTTING CONTEST, SO OUR CEO WILL DO YOUR JOB FOR A DAY.

I FEEL LIKE A FAILURE...DARKNESS FILLS MY DAYS...I DREAM OF THE GRAVE.

THIS IS LESS MOTIVATING THAN I'D HOPED.

I'LL NEVER BE LOVED AGAIN!!

I'LL DESIGN THE SYSTEM AS SOON AS YOU GIVE ME THE USER REQUIREMENTS.

BETTER YET, YOU COULD BUILD THE SYSTEM, THEN I'LL TELL YOUR BOSS THAT IT DOESN'T MEET MY NEEDS.

I DON'T MEAN TO FRIGHTEN YOU, BUT YOU'LL HAVE TO DO SOME ACTUAL WORK.

THAT'S CRAZY TALK.

I CAN'T START THE PROJECT BECAUSE THE USER WON'T GIVE ME HIS REQUIREMENTS.

START MAKING SOMETHING ANYWAY. OTHERWISE WE'LL LOOK UNHELPFUL.

SO, OUR PLAN IS TO CLEVERLY HIDE OUR COMPETENCE.

YOU THINK TOO MUCH.

THERE'S NO BUDGET FOR YOUR PROJECT; YOU NEED TO TIN-CUP IT.

WHAT?

BE LIKE A BEGGAR AND ASK EACH DEPARTMENT TO GIVE YOU A BIT OF THEIR BUDGET.

WELL, NOW THAT YOU'VE LAUGHED YOUR GUTS OUT, DO YOU FEEL BETTER?

ERK!

THEY BELIEVE IN FENG SHUI. THEY BELIEVE IN THE PET PSYCHIC.

THIS SUGGESTS AN EXCELLENT NEW CAREER FOR ME.

THE FURNITURE PSYCHIC IS HERE. HE SAYS MY WASTEBASKET IS IN LOVE WITH MY DESK.

FURNITURE PSYCHIC

YOUR OLD CHAIR HAS PASSED TO THE OTHER SIDE.

HE SAYS YOU'LL KNOW WHAT THIS MEANS: "SQUEAK, SQUEAK."

YES

YOUR DESK SAYS, "THANKS FOR THE GUM."

I NEED CLOSURE!

OUR CEO WILL BE JOINING US IN A MINUTE.

AS USUAL, HE'LL BE MAKING AN AWKWARD ATTEMPT TO SEEM LIKE "JUST PLAIN FOLK."

EXCUSE ME — IS THIS ORDINARY CHAIR AVAILABLE FOR AN AVERAGE GUY LIKE ME?

I'LL ROLL UP MY SLEEVES AND GET TO WORK. I'M NOT TOO GOOD FOR REAL WORK.

I HAVE A SECRETARY, BUT IT'S ALMOST AS IF I WORK FOR HER. HA HA! IT'S IRONIC.

LAST WEEKEND I WORE BLUE JEANS AND DROVE A TRACTOR!

SIR, YOUR HELICOPTER IS HERE TO TAKE YOU TO YOUR ISLAND FORTRESS FOR THE FOX HUNT.

ITTY BITTY FOR-TRESS

THE INTERNS ARE ALREADY IN FULL FOX COSTUMES.

3/30/03 ©2003 United Feature Syndicate, Inc.

SHE'S PARANOID ABOUT NOT BEING INVITED TO MEET-INGS. CAN YOU FIX HER?

NOPE.

CAN I TRADE HER IN?

WOULD YOU LIKE A LIAR, A MORON, OR A WHISTLER?

YOU CAN'T REPAIR A DEFECTIVE CO-WORKER.

THE BEST YOU CAN DO IS TRADE FOR A CO-WORKER WHOSE DEFECTS YOU HAVEN'T YET DISCOVERED.

WHAT'S WRONG WITH THIS ONE?

HE PARTS HIS HAIR IN THE MIDDLE; THAT'S JUST WRONG.

CAROL, THIS IS OUR NEW GUY, HARRY MIDDLEPART.

I DON'T APPROVE OF YOUR HAIR-STYLE. I FORBID YOU TO BE NEAR MY WORKSPACE.

SHE'S NOT GOOD PEOPLE.

THE SEVENTIES CALLED. THEY WANT THEIR HAIR BACK!!

OUR VP IS MAD BECAUSE PEOPLE ARE LEAVING WORK TOO EARLY.

IF YOU NEED TO LEAVE EARLY, DON'T WALK PAST HIS OFFICE. GO TO THE ROOF AND LEAP INTO THE "DUMPSTER" IN THE ALLEY.

LEADERSHIP TRIUMPHS AGAIN.

A CO-WORKER WHO SHALL REMAIN NAMELESS HAS ACCUSED YOU OF UNSPECIFIED SHORTCOMINGS.

YOUR ACCUSER HAS BEEN PLACED IN THE WITNESS PROTECTION PROGRAM.

YOU HAVE A PROGRAM FOR THAT?

ACTUALLY, I JUST FORGET WHO SAYS WHAT.

ASOK, YOUR WORK HAS BEEN EXCELLENT ALL YEAR.

I'M RATING YOU "POOR" SO I'LL HAVE A PAPER TRAIL IN CASE I EVER NEED TO FIRE YOU.

YOU'LL PROBABLY FEEL A LITTLE SURGE OF MOTIVATION BECAUSE YOU GOT FEEDBACK.

I THINK MY HEAD IS GETTING HEAVIER FROM ALL THE NEW THOUGHTS.

I PLAN TO COMPENSATE BY PROPPING IT UP WITH MY ARM DURING MEETINGS.

SOME PEOPLE THINK YOU HAVE NO GOALS.

LONG TERM, I HOPE TO BE ON A STAMP.

5/5/03 © 2003 United Feature Syndicate, Inc.

ELBONIA HAS GOTTEN A BAD REPUTATION. WE NEED YOUR HELP TO REBUILD OUR IMAGE.

THE PROBLEM BEGAN WHEN WE DISCOVERED A CIVILIZATION OF LEPRECHAUNS LIVING UNDER OUR MUD.

NOW THEY'RE OUR PRIMARY EXPORT. BUT WE UNDERESTIMATED THE VEGETARIAN BACKLASH.

5/6/03 © 2003 United Feature Syndicate, Inc.

P.R. FOR ELBONIA

THE MEDIA GIVE YOU A BAD RAP FOR EXPORTING LEPRECHAUN MEAT.

OUR AD CAMPAIGN WILL FEATURE A LEPRECHAUN EXPLAINING THAT THEY ENJOY BEING EATEN.

ELBONIANS ARE OUR BEST FRIENDS. NOW EXCUSE ME WHILE I TENDERIZE MYSELF.

5/7/03 © 2003 United Feature Syndicate, Inc.

122

ALICE MOVED INTO THE CORNER CUBICLE AND CLAIMED CONTROL OVER THE WINDOW SHADES!

GAAA!!

OUR LIFE SUPPORT SYSTEMS WILL BE IN THE HANDS OF A MAD-WOMAN!

MAYBE SHE'LL BE KIND.

ALICE, I UNDERSTAND YOU'VE BEEN USING A GIANT MAGNIFYING GLASS AS A DEATH RAY IN THE OFFICE.

IT'S NOT A DEATH RAY. I USE IT ONLY TO BURN OFF TOUPEES.

OH... THAT'S OKAY.

IS YOUR HEAD TOO WARM? MY HEAD IS TOO WARM.

QUESTION: HOW DO YOU KNOW WHICH MANAGEMENT TECHNIQUES WORK BEST?

LOGICALLY, DOESN'T THE EXISTENCE OF THOUSANDS OF MANAGEMENT BOOKS SHOW THAT NO ONE KNOWS WHAT WORKS BEST?

THE TRICK IS KNOWING WHICH ONE TO READ.

NOW YOU'RE JUST MAKING ME MAD.

I JUST REALIZED THAT MY CAREER PRIMARILY CONSISTS OF ASKING YOU FOR STUFF...

...AND WONDERING HOW LONG I SHOULD WAIT BEFORE I REMIND YOU.

DO YOU KNOW HOW THAT MAKES ME FEEL?

HOW WHAT MAKES YOU FEEL?

WE CAN'T AFFORD TO HIRE QUALIFIED EMPLOYEES.

MY PLAN IS TO HIRE DUMB PEOPLE AND BE ANGRY AT THEM.

I FORGET — WHAT'S THE WORD FOR PRETENDING THAT PEOPLE CAN CHANGE THEIR BASIC NATURE?

MOTIVA-TION?

LONG TERM, I HOPE TO CONVINCE OUR BOSS THAT I HAVE THE POWER TO BECOME INVISIBLE.

THEN I CAN JUST SIT HOME AND GET PAID. OH, IT WILL BE SWEET.

WALLY? IS THAT YOU?

RIGHT IN FRONT OF YOU.